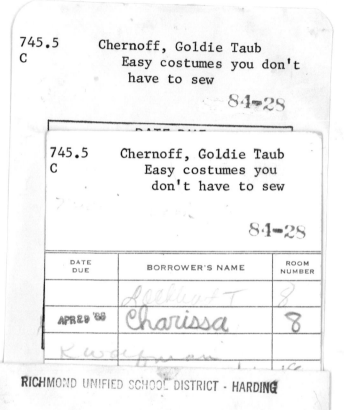

745.5
C

Chernoff, Goldie Taub
Easy costumes you don't
have to sew

84-28

745.5
C

Chernoff, Goldie Taub
Easy costumes you
don't have to sew

84-28

DATE DUE	BORROWER'S NAME	ROOM NUMBER
	Leekleaf T	8
APR 29 '88	Charissa	8
	K waefman	

3-6

EASY COSTUMES
you don't have to sew

EASY COSTUMES
you don't have to sew

by Goldie Taub Chernoff

Costumes designed
and illustrated by
Margaret A. Hartelius

FOUR WINDS PRESS 🍃 NEW YORK

CAUTION: Since most of these costumes are made from paper, we do not recommend their use without proper supervision. Children should be warned to keep away from flame.

Library of Congress Cataloging in Publication Data

Chernoff, Goldie Taub.
    Easy costumes you don't have to sew.

    Summary: Instructions for easily constructed costumes which do not require sewing.
    1. Costume — Juvenile literature. 2. Paper work — Juvenile literature. [1. Costume. 2. Paper work]
    I. Hartelius, Margaret A. II. Title.
TT633.C48   745.54   76-46428
ISBN 0-590-07491-1

Published by Four Winds Press
A Division of Scholastic Magazines, Inc., New York, N.Y.
Text copyright© 1975 by Goldie Taub Chernoff
Illustrations copyright© 1975 by Margaret A. Hartelius
All rights reserved
Printed in the United States of America
Library of Congress Catalog Card number: 76-46428

3 4 5   81 80 79 78

For Gabriel Morgan Steinfeld

EASY COSTUMES
you don't have to sew

A Stuffed Tomato

All of the costumes in this section are made from a basic sack which is stapled and then stuffed to give it roundness. Accessories are then added to create the final effect. Using this simple approach, you can create a variety of characters in addition to those shown in this book.

**To make the Stuffed Tomato
you will need:**

a large piece of red cloth, newspaper, a stapler, ribbon, a grocery bag large enough to fit on the head, colored paper or poster paint.

The Basic Sack

Measure a length of cloth as wide as the distance from elbow to elbow with arms extended, and twice as long as the distance from neck to knees.

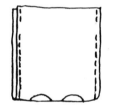

Fold the material in half, with the wrong side out. Staple the sides together leaving holes for the arms as shown. Cut 2 holes out of the bottom fold for the legs to go through.

Turn the sack right side out. Make slits, at intervals, near the top and thread a ribbon or string through the slits. Put the sack aside and make the accessories.

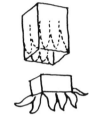

The Accessories

Cut leaf or petal shapes all around the open end of a paper bag.

Decorate with green paint or colored paper.

To put on the costume:

Have the child step into the sack. Stuff the sack with shredded or crumpled newspaper until it is round and full.

Pull the ribbon to gather the sack at the neck and tie.

Put the petal hat on the child's head.

A Snowman

To make the Snowman you will need:

an old white sheet, ribbon or heavy cord, a grocery bag large enough to fit over the head, construction paper, white glue, tape, a stapler, newspaper.

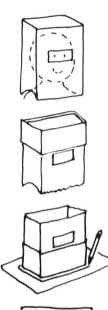

The Snowman's mask and hat

Cut an eye opening in the middle of one side of the grocery bag as shown.

Glue or tape black paper to the top part of the bag above the eye opening as shown. (This will be the crown of the hat.)

Cover the rest of the bag with white paper. Do not cover the eye opening.

Now make a brim for the hat. Place the bag on a large sheet of black paper. Using the bottom of the bag as a guide, cut a hole in the center of the black paper. Now you have a brim. Slip it over the bag and tape it in place.

Cut a long narrow triangle out of orange paper for a nose. Fold and tape in place.

Cut circles out of black paper for eyes and mouth. Glue them in place.

The Snowman's body

Make a basic sack out of the old white sheet. (See page 3.)

Staple or glue black paper circles down the front.

To put on the costume:

Have the child step into the sack. Stuff the sack as described on page 3. Pull the ribbon to gather the sack at the neck and tie.

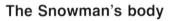

Put the mask on the child. Tie a scarf around the neck. Add boots, mittens, and an old broom.

A Fat Mouse

To make the Fat Mouse you will need:

an old white sheet for the body, a paper plate for the mask, construction paper, pink ribbon, newspaper, tape, white glue, stapler, string.

The Mask

Cut eye holes out of a paper plate to fit the child's eyes.

Poke a hole on each side of the plate and tie strings through the holes.

Cut a semicircle out of white paper. Overlap the ends to form a cone. Staple the cone together.

Tape the cone to the plate as shown.

Cut paper strips for whiskers and a piece of pink paper for a nose. Tape them to the tip of the cone.

Cut 2 large round ears out of paper. Tape, glue, or staple them in place.

Draw or paint a mouth on the underside of the cone.

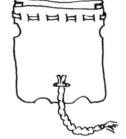

The Body

Make a basic sack out of the old white sheet. (See page 3.)

Make a tail out of braided pink ribbon or yarn.

Pin or staple the tail to the back of the sack.

To put on the costume:

Have the child step into the sack. Stuff the sack as described on page 3, but do not use as much stuffing. The Mouse should be thinner than the Tomato or the Snowman.

Tie the sack at the neck.

Put the mask on the child and tie it in place.

White or pink gloves and socks will complete the costume.

A Shaggy Dog

The costumes in this section are made from paper bags. The basic unit for each costume is a large grocery bag the child can slip into and wear as a body covering. Other parts are made from paper or cardboard and then attached to the bag.

To make the Shaggy Dog you will need:

2 large grocery bags for the body and mask, a small paper lunch bag for the nose, newspaper, construction paper, a stapler, white glue, scotch tape, lightweight cardboard for the tail.

The Body

Cut a slit up the back of 1 bag. Cut neck and arm holes.

For the dog's fur, fold a sheet of newspaper in half and cut fringe along the open side.

Now tape the fringe around the bag, starting at the open end. Repeat the process until the bag is covered with overlapping rows of fringe.

Cut a tail out of lightweight cardboard. Tape newspaper fringe to the tail.

Staple the tail to the back of the bag as shown.

The Head

Cut an eye opening in the other large grocery bag about three inches from the top.

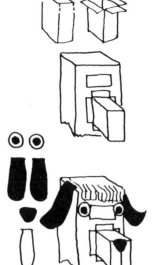

Use the small lunch bag for the nose piece. Cut a slit in each corner of the bag and fold back to make tabs as shown.

Glue or tape the tabs in place on the large bag under the eye opening.

Cut large eyes and ears out of paper and glue them in place.

Cut more paper fringe. Glue to the top of the bag at the front and back as shown.

Cut a big black nose and a long red tongue out of paper. Glue them in place.

Cut 4 paws, larger than the child's hands, out of construction paper or brown paper. Staple 2 of the paws together to form a mitt.

To put on the costume:

Have the child put on the body bag and tape the back closed.

Put the mask over the child's head. If necessary, trim the bag at the bottom so that the eye opening is in the right place. Slip the paw mitts on the child's hands.

Make the Shaggy Dog's costume body and paw mitts (see page 9), but use 3 old nylon stockings braided together for the tail. (Tie the 3 stockings together at the heels and then braid.) Staple the tail to the back of the costume.

A Scary Lion

The Head

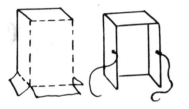

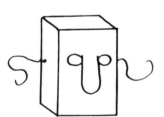

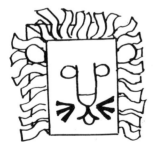

Use a cereal box large enough to cover the child's face.

Cut away the 4 flaps at the open end of the box.

Cut away the back of the box.

Cover the outside of the box with yellow construction paper.

Poke holes in each side and tie strings through.

Cut eye holes in the front of the box.

Cut a nose shape as shown.

For a mane, cut orange construction or tissue paper into strips. Glue or tape strips all around the box.

Add paper ears. Draw or paint a mouth and tongue.

Glue on paper strips for whiskers.

A Furry Gorilla

Make the Shaggy Dog's costume body, (see page 9).
Add a gorilla mask and 4 large hands (see below).

Use a luncheon-size paper plate and cut out eye holes.
Poke holes in each side of the plate and tie strings through.

Staple a larger paper plate to the small plate just below the eyes as shown.

Paint on a nose and mouth.

Cut ears out of paper. Glue on.

Glue on fringed paper for hair.

The Mask

The Hands

Cut 4 large hands out of lightweight cardboard.

Cut openings for the child's ankles in two of the hands as shown.

Put these hands around the child's ankles over his sneakers.

Poke 2 holes in each hand where the sneaker laces tie. Pull the laces through the holes and tie them.

Have the child wear a long-sleeved shirt under the costume. Pin the other pair of hands to the cuffs of the shirt.

A Big Green Frog

**To make the Big Green Frog
you will need:**

2 large grocery bags for the body and
mask, lightweight cardboard for the
hands and feet, construction paper,
white glue, tape, a stapler, poster paint,
string.

The Mask

Cut an eye opening in one of the grocery bags.

Cut 2 mouth pieces, shaped as shown, out of green construction paper. (One piece should be smaller than the other.)

Fold the sides of the mouth pieces back to form tabs and glue the tabs in place on the bag. Place the smaller one above the eye opening as shown.

Cut large eyes out of paper. Fold the paper back to make tabs at the bottom. Glue the eyes to the top of the bag.

Paint dots on the bag.

The Hands and Feet

Cut 2 large hands out of lightweight cardboard.

Poke 2 holes in each hand.

Now cut 2 large frog feet out of the cardboard. Cut openings for the child's ankles in the feet as shown.

Paint the hands and feet green.

The Body

Cut a slit up the back of the other grocery bag. Cut neck and arm holes.

Cut a circle out of yellow paper large enough to cover the front of the bag.

Glue the circle to the front of the bag.

Cut spots out of yellow and green paper and glue them all over the bag.

To put on the costume:

Put the body part on the child and tape the back closed. (If possible have the child wear a green sweater and tights under the costume.)

Tie the large hands to the child's wrists with string or ribbon.

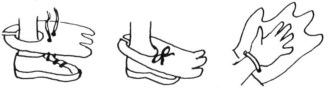

Put the feet around the child's ankles over the sneakers. Poke two holes in the cardboard where the sneaker laces tie. Pull the laces through and tie.

Turn the tips of the feet up slightly to prevent tripping.

Put the mask over the child's head.

A Monster Lobster

To make the Monster Lobster you will need:

3 large grocery bags (one for the body, one for the tail, one for the mask), construction paper, lightweight cardboard, white glue, tape, a stapler.

The Mask

Cut an eye opening in one of the bags. Cut off corners.

Cut 2 large triangle shapes out of heavy brown paper or lightweight cardboard. The bases of the triangles should be as wide as the bag.

Glue or tape the triangles to the top of the head, one in front and the other in the back, as shown.

Staple or tape the tops of the triangles together.

Cut 2 large eyes out of cardboard. Glue or staple them in place.

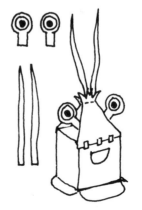

Cut long feelers out of cardboard. Staple them to the top of the triangles.

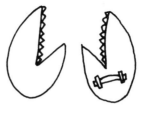

The Claws

Cut 2 large claws out of lightweight cardboard.

Tape a strip of paper to the underside of each claw to hold it in place on the child's hand as shown.

The Body

Cut a slit up the front of the second bag. Cut neck and arm holes.

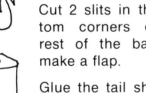

The Tail

Cut away the front of the third bag.

Use this front piece to cut out a tail shape as shown.

Cut 2 slits in the bottom corners of the rest of the bag and make a flap.

Glue the tail shape to this flap.

Tape or glue the tail assembly to the back of the body bag.

FRONT   BACK

To put on the costume:

Put the body assembly on the child and tape the front closed.

Cut a large oval out of light green paper. Tape it to the front of the costume.

Put the mask on the child. Tape the mask to the body section to give it stability.

Slip the claws on the child's hands. (Note: The whole costume can be painted green, or parts of it covered with green construction paper.)

A Turtle

Sandwich boards are particularly useful when you need a quick, effective costume and time is short. All you need for the basics are 2 large pieces of cardboard which can be decorated, painted, or shaped in any way you wish.

To make the Turtle you will need:

2 large pieces of cardboard or 2 sheets of oaktag, a large grocery bag, construction paper, heavy string or ribbon, white glue, a stapler.

The Body

Cut 2 large circles. Paint a shell design on each.

Poke 2 holes at the top of each circle. Tie the circles together to make a sandwich board.

Staple a tail to the bottom of the back circle.

Have the child wear a turtleneck sweater under the shell.

The Head

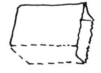

Cut away one of the narrow sides of the grocery bag.

Glue green construction paper to the remainder of the bag.

Glue a large eye on each side of the head. Draw on a mouth and scales.

Poke a hole on each side of the head and tie a ribbon on.

A Ladybug

To make the Ladybug you will need:

2 large pieces of cardboard or oaktag, heavy string, construction paper, pipe cleaners, a stapler, tape.

The Body

Cut 2 large circles out of the cardboard.

Paint the circles red with black dots.

Poke 2 holes at the top of each circle. Tie the circles together to make a sand-wich board as shown.

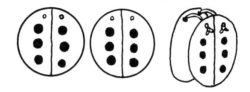

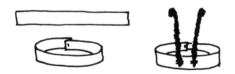

The Headdress

Cut a 2″ band out of con-struction paper large enough to go around the child's head with an over-lap of about 1″.

Staple the band together.

Staple pipe cleaners to the front of the band.

The Eye Mask

Cut a piece of black paper into a 3″ × 6″ strip.

Fold the strip in half and cut as shown.

Tape the eye mask to the head band.

A Big Bat

Plastic trash bags are ideal to use for costumes. They are sturdy, can be cut or stapled, and come in a variety of sizes and colors. In addition, they are easy to draw on if you use felt markers. By cutting the bags in different ways and adding various elements, which can be taped on securely with transparent tape, you can create a surprising variety of simple but effective costumes.

To make the Bat you will need:

a lawn-and-leaf size black plastic trash bag, lightweight cardboard, a stapler, tape, construction paper, string.

The Mask

Use a 9 × 12″ sheet of black construction paper. Fold it in half the long way.

Cut out the ear and eye shapes as shown.

Open the mask and poke a hole in each side.

Thread a knotted string through each hole.

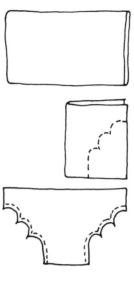

The Body

Hold the trash bag horizontally.

Fold it in half. Cut out the shape shown.

Now open the bag. Lay it flat. Staple the side seams together.

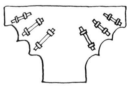

Cut 6 strips of cardboard — two 6″ × 1″; two 9″ × 1″; and two 12″ × 1″. Tape the cardboard strips to the wings as shown. This is the front of the costume.

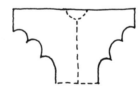

Turn the costume over and cut a neck opening and a slit down the back. Also slit the bottom of the costume open.

To put on the costume:

Have the child put his or her arms in the wings. Tape the costume closed in the back. Put the mask on and tie it in place.

A Giant Chicken

To make the Giant Chicken you will need:

a tall, kitchen-can size plastic bag (either yellow or white), construction paper, tape, a large grocery bag, white glue, lightweight cardboard, felt markers or paint, string.

The Body

Cut neck and arm holes in the plastic bag.

Cut a slit up the back of the bag.

For feathers, fold 9″ × 12″ sheets of brown and orange construction paper in quarters and cut out shapes as shown.

Cut fringe on the sides of the "feathers."

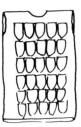

Now lay the bag flat with the front side up. Starting at the top of the bag, tape alternating brown and orange feathers in rows until the front is covered. Turn the bag over and repeat until the back is covered.

The Wings and Feet

Make wings out of lightweight cardboard. Poke 2 holes at the top of each wing and 2 at the bottom.

Cut 2 big chicken feet out of cardboard.

Cut ankle holes in them as shown.

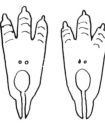

The Mask

Cut an eye opening in one of the narrow sides of the grocery bag as shown.

Cut scallops along the bottom of the bag.

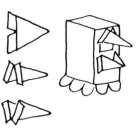

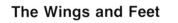

Cut 2 triangles for the chicken's beak out of yellow construction paper. Fold and glue the beak to the bag as shown.

Cut a large comb and wattles out of red construction paper. Fold and glue in place.

Cut 2 large eyes out of paper. Glue one to each side of the bag. Draw or paint feathers on the mask.

To put on the costume:

Put the body bag on the child and tape the back closed.

Tie the wings on the child's arms with string or ribbon at the shoulders and wrists.

Put the feet around the child's ankles over the shoes. Poke 2 holes for the laces to tie through. Pull the laces through and tie.

Then put on the mask.

A Bony Skeleton

To make the Skeleton you will need:

a lawn-and-leaf size black plastic bag, heavy white paper, a stapler, tape, a paper plate, felt marker, string.

The Mask

Cut eye holes in the paper plate and draw heavy black outlines around them with the marker. Draw a nose.

Poke holes in each side of the mask and tie strings through.

For a mouth, cut a strip of paper and draw on teeth.

Fold the ends of the strip forward. Staple the strip to the mask as shown so that the mouth piece curves out.

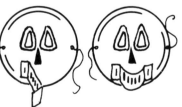

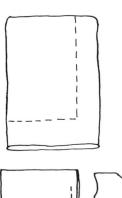

The Skeleton's Body

Cut the bag down in both width and length to fit the child. The bag should be just wide enough to fit without any fullness and it should hang just below the child's knees.

After you have cut the bag to size, staple the seam together on the cut side, leaving a space at the top for 1 arm hole.

Cut the other arm hole in the other side of the bag.

Cut a hole in the top for the neck and slit the costume down the back.

Now cut out the bone parts from the heavy white paper as follows: Cut out 7 oval shapes for the spine, 6 strips for the ribs, 8 large bones for the arms and legs, and a large heart shape for the pelvic bone.

Put aside 4 of the large bones to be used when the costume is put on.

Lay the bag flat, front side up, and tape the rest of the bone parts on as shown.

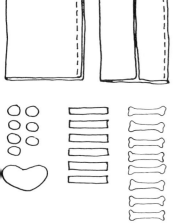

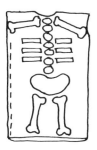

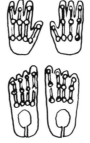

Cut 2 large hands and 2 large feet out of lightweight cardboard.

To put on the costume:

Have the child wear black pants and a black sweater under the costume.

Put the costume on the child and tape the back closed.

Now get the 4 large bones you put aside earlier. Tape 2 of the bones to the child's sweater sleeves and the other 2 bones to the pants as shown.

Pin the skeleton hands to the cuffs of the sweater sleeves. Put the skeleton feet around the child's ankles. Poke 2 holes where the shoelaces tie. Pull the laces through and tie the skeleton feet in place.

Put the mask on and tie it in place.

A Robot

Cartons are ideal to use when certain types of costumes are required. Such things as airplanes, cars, or robots lend themselves well to this type of costume construction.

To make the Robot you will need:

a carton large enough to fit over the child's body and come down to the waist, a smaller box or carton that will fit over the child's head, 3 paper cups, wire, tape, cardboard, white glue, paper fasteners.

The Head

Cut an eye opening in one side of the smaller box.

Glue or tape paper cups to the box for a nose and for the ears as shown.

Cut large eyes out of paper and glue in place.

Poke a hole in the top of the box and push a wire through for an antenna.

Loop the wire and tape it in place on the inside of the box.

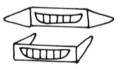

For the mouth piece, cut a strip of cardboard wider than the box. Fold the ends of the strip back for tabs.

Attach the tabs to the sides of the box with paper fasteners.

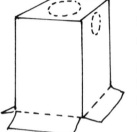

The Body

Cut away the flaps at the open end of the carton.

At the other end of the carton, cut a hole large enough to go over the child's head.

Cut arm holes in the sides of the carton.

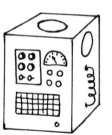

Now decorate the carton. Draw on a control board and add three-dimensional parts made from old buttons, wires, gear parts, pipe cleaners, pictures from magazines, etc.

A Totem Pole

**To make the Totem Pole
you will need:**

a large carton for the base, paint, several boxes of different sizes for the tower, construction paper, tape, white glue.

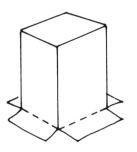

The Base

Use a carton big enough to fit over the child's head and reach the waist.

Cut away the flaps at the open end of the carton.

At the other end of the carton, cut a hole large enough to fit over the child's head.

Cut holes for the child's arms.

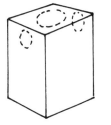

Decorate all the boxes with a totem pole design.

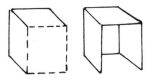

The Tower

Get a smaller box that will fit over the child's head. Cut away one side of the box to make an opening for the child's face.

Glue another box to the top of this box, and still another to the top of that one.

To put on the costume:

Have the child put the base carton on first.

Put the tower on the child's head. Tape the tower to the base carton for stability.

A Fiery Dragon Costume for a Group

To make the Dragon you will need:

a carton for each child in the group (large enough to come down over the head and cover the hips), a shallower carton for the Dragon's head, newspaper, heavy cord, cardboard, tape, white glue, paint, a styrofoam ball.

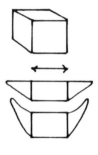

The Dragon's Head

Use the shallower carton. (This will later be glued on top of the front carton of the Dragon's body.)

Cut 2 jaw pieces—as wide as the carton—out of light-weight cardboard, as shown.

Fold the side tabs back and tape or glue them to the carton.

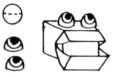

Cut a styrofoam ball in half. Paint an eye on each half. Glue the eyes to the top of the box.

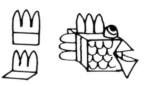

Cut 2 fin shapes out of cardboard. Fold the fins at the bottom for tabs. Glue the tabs to the top and back of the head.

Cut teeth and a tongue out of paper and glue them in place.

Paint scales on the sides of the head.

The Body Sections

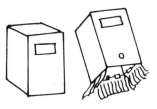

Cut slits in the front side of each carton as shown.

Cut fringe from newspaper and tape it around the bottom of each carton on the inside.

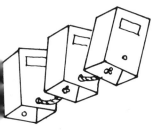

Now poke a hole in the front and back of each carton and link the cartons together with pieces of knotted cord.

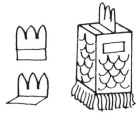

Cut fin shapes for the Dragon's back out of lightweight cardboard. Cut a shape for each carton, except one. Fold the fins at the bottom to make tabs. Glue the tabs to the tops of the cartons as shown.

Paint scales on all the cartons.

Tape and glue the head to the front body section.

The Tail

Cut 5 tail sections out of cardboard as shown.

Poke holes in each section, top and bottom. Tie the sections loosely together with cord.

Fold back part of the front of the tail and glue it to the end of the Dragon.

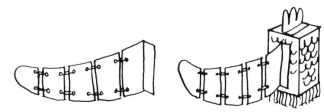

Hats

Sometimes all you need is a hat to create a special character. A long cape, leotards, or imagination can do the rest. Here are a variety of effective hats made from a few basic patterns. The hats can stand on their own or serve as points of departure for creating the rest of the costume.

PAPER BAND HATS

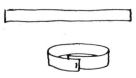

The Basic Band

Cut a 2"-wide strip of paper long enough to go around the head with an overlap of about 1". Staple ends together.

INDIAN HEADDRESS

Make a basic band.

Tape or staple real or paper feathers to the band.

ROYAL CROWN

Make a basic band about 4" wide.

Cut points in the top.

Decorate the crown with beads, buttons, braids, sparkles, etc.

POLICEMAN HAT

Make a 4" band.

Cut a crescent moon shape out of paper for a visor. Tape the visor to the band.

Cut a badge out of colored paper and glue it in place.

CONE HATS

The Basic Cone

Fold a 12″ × 24″ sheet of newspaper in half.

Cut out a quarter circle and open the paper into a half circle.

Roll the half circle into a cone to fit the head. Tape or staple the cone together.

CLOWN HAT

Make a basic cone.

Paint the cone with bright colors.

Add pompons, bells, or ribbons.

CHINESE HAT

Fold an 18″ × 18″ sheet of paper in half and then in half again.

Draw a quarter circle and cut it out.

Open the paper out into a full circle.

Cut a slit to the center. Now bring the open ends together so that they overlap about 2″ and tape the hat closed.

WITCH HAT

Make the basic cone out of black paper.

Now make the brim. Place the cone on a sheet of stiff paper and draw around it.

Draw a larger circle around the first circle and cut it out.

Draw 5 tabs inside the inner circle as shown.

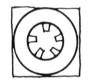

Cut out the inner circle around the tabs.

Fold the tabs back.

Slip the brim over the cone and glue to tape the tabs to the cone as shown.

PILGRIM HAT

First make a witch's hat.

Cut off about one third of the cone from the top.

Cut a buckle out of paper. Glue the buckle to the hat band. Save the tip of the cone for a nose.

TUBE HATS

The Basic Tube

Make a tube out of heavy paper or lightweight cardboard large enough to go around the head with an overlap of about 1". Tape the tube closed.

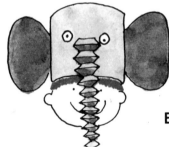

ELEPHANT HAT

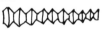

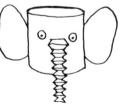

Make a basic tube.

Cut 2 big, floppy ears out of construction paper.

Glue the ears to each side of the tube.

For the trunk, cut a long narrow triangle out of paper. Fold it accordion style as shown.

Glue the trunk to the front of the tube.

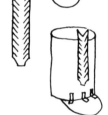

BAND LEADER HAT

Make a basic tube.

Cut fringe along both sides of a long paper strip to make a feather.

Glue the feather to the front of the tube.

Cut a crescent moon shape from paper for a visor. Tape the visor in place.

SENTRY HAT

Make a basic tube.

Fringe one side of long strips of construction paper or tissue paper.

Starting at the bottom of the tube, tape the fringed strips in rows.

Staple or tie ribbon to each side of the tube for a chin strap.

MILK CARTON HATS

KNIGHT'S HELMET

You will need 2 one-gallon milk cartons, paper fasteners.

The Visor

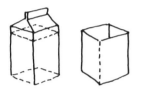

Remove the bottom and top of one of the milk cartons. Use the middle section.

Slit one side and flatten the carton. You will now have 4 sections.

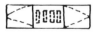

Cut a strip 3″ wide across three of these sections.

Mark and cut eye slits in the center section of the strip. Cut points at both ends.

The Helmet

Remove the bottom and front of the other milk carton.

Attach the visor to the helmet with paper fasteners.

Add a paper plume to the top of the helmet.

PAPER BAG HATS

BONNET

Cut away the front of a flatbottomed grocery bag.

Fold the remaining 3 sides back a little to form a cuff.

Decorate the bonnet with rickrack, paper flowers, lace, etc.

Poke a hole on each side of the bonnet and tie ribbons through.

(Note: Add paper ears to make a Rabbit's Easter Bonnet.)

JESTER'S CAP

Cut petal shapes around the open end of a bag.

Cut away the bottom of the bag.

Paint vertical stripes of color on all sides.

Sew or tape light, round plastic buttons or bells to the end of each petal.

Pleated Paper

Paper, in all colors, folded in accordion pleats is extremely versatile and can be used to create a variety of accessories and costumes.

Accordion fold 9″ × 12″ sheets of construction paper.

Staple one end to form a fan.

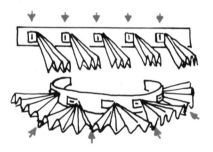

Staple the fans at 3″ intervals on a strip of paper. (The length of the strip will depend on what you will use the pleated paper for.)

Join the fans with staples as shown.

Use pleated paper for:

A TUTU

A PARASOL

A COLLAR

WINGS

TAILS

A HEADDRESS

Quick Disguises

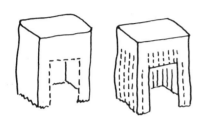

AN EGG CARTON MASK

Cut away 2 adjoining cup sections from an egg carton. Cut holes for the eyes in the bottom of each cup. Poke a hole on each side and tie strings through. Tie the mask on.

A PAPER BAG WIG

Use a flat-bottomed bag large enough to fit over the child's head.

Cut away about ¾ of the front section of the bag for the face opening. Fringe the remaining ¼ for bangs.

Fringe the bottom of the bag all the way around. Curl the fringed ends around a pencil.

A CURLY BEARD

Fold a 9″ × 12″ piece of construction paper in half. Fringe along the open side almost to the fold.

Curl the fringe by pulling it over the sharp edge of a scissors blade.

Poke a hole in each side of the beard at the top. Tie strings in the holes. Fasten at the back of the head or loop over the ears. Add a mustache.

MUSTACHES

Fold construction paper in half. Draw a half of any mustache shape along the fold.

Cut out the shape and open the paper.

Tape the mustache to the upper lip or cut a nose hook as shown.

Fringe the bottom of the mustache if you wish.

FOLDED PAPER MASKS

Use a piece of construction paper large enough to cover the child's eyes and nose.

Fold the paper in half. Draw shapes as shown, or draw any shape you wish, and cut it out.

Leave paper folded and cut out an eye hole.

Open the mask. Poke holes in each side and tie strings through.

Tie the mask on.

NOSES

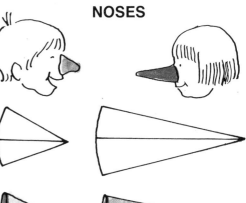

Cut a triangle out of construction paper as shown.

Fold the triangle down the middle and attach it to the child's nose with masking tape.

Mix and Match

Plastic Bag Body of
Giant Chicken +
Knight's Helmet =

White Garbage Bag + Paper Stars +
Pleated Paper + Paper Tube Torch =

Basic Sack +
Clown Hat +
Pleated Paper =

Lobster Body +
Frog Mask =

Knight in Armor

Statue of Liberty

Fat Clown

Lady Bug Mask +
Sandwich Board
with Stripes +
Paper Wings =

Basic Sack +
Elephant Hat =

Strange Fish

A Bee

Elephant